Read About
Kobe Bryant

David P. Torsiello

Enslow Elementary
an imprint of
Enslow Publishers, Inc.
40 Industrial Road
Box 398
Berkeley Heights, NJ 07922
USA

http://www.enslow.com

For Mr. Troyano: My love of books was born in your classroom.

Enslow Elementary, an imprint of Enslow Publishers, Inc.

Enslow Elementary® is a registered trademark of Enslow Publishers, Inc.

Library of Congress Cataloging-in-Publication Data

Torsiello, David P.
  Read about Kobe Bryant / David P. Torsiello.
       p. cm. — (I like sports stars!)
  Includes bibliographical references and index.
  Summary: "Kobe Bryant is the star player for the Los Angeles Lakers. He has gained much fame over the years for his sensational play and the championships he has won. He hopes to continue winning many more in the future"—Provided by publisher.
  ISBN 978-0-7660-3830-1
  1. Bryant, Kobe, 1979-—Juvenile literature. 2. Basketball players—United States—Biography--Juvenile literature. 3. Los Angeles Lakers (Basketball team)—Juvenile literature. I. Title.
  GV884.B794T68 2011
  796.323092—dc23
  [B]
                                    2011020414
Paperback ISBN: 978-1-59845-300-3

Printed in the United States of America

062011 Lake Book Manufacturing, Inc., Melrose Park, IL

10 9 8 7 6 5 4 3 2 1

♻ Enslow Publishers, Inc., is committed to printing our books on recycled paper. The paper in every book contains 10% to 30% post-consumer waste (PCW). The cover board on the outside of each book contains 100% PCW. Our goal is to do our part to help young people and the environment too!

Every effort has been made to locate all copyright holders of material used in this book. If any errors or omissions have occurred, corrections will be made in future editions of this book.

Photo Credits: AP Images/Branimir Kvartuc, p. 7; AP Images/Chris Pizzello, p. 11; AP Images/Danny Moloshok, p. 20–21; AP Images/David J. Phillip, p. 22; AP Images/Dusan Vranic, p. 21; AP Images/Frank Franklin II, p. 13; AP/Kevork Djansezian, pp. 16, 23; AP Images/Mark Avery, p. 12; AP Images/Mark J. Terrill, pp. 1, 4, 15, 18; AP Images/Michael Caulfield, pp. 8, 10, 17; AP Images/Ralph Freso, p. 14; AP Images/Rich Pedroncelli, p. 19; AP Images/Rusty Kennedy, p. 9.

Cover Illustration: AP Images/Mark J. Terrill

CONTENTS

WORDS TO KNOW

defense—Keeping the other team from scoring.

dribble—When you bounce the ball off the floor with your fingertips.

rebound—Grabbing the ball after a missed shot.

shooting guard—One of the positions on a basketball team.

Kobe Bryant was born August 23, 1978. He is the star player for the Los Angeles Lakers.

Kobe's father, Joe Bryant, was also a basketball player. Joe Bryant's nickname was Jellybean!

Kobe was a great
player in high school.
He was so good he
went straight to the
pros.

Kobe joined the Lakers in 1996. He had a very good first year with the team.

Kobe plays shooting guard.
A shooting guard must know
how to dribble and shoot the ball.

Kobe can also play
defense and rebound.

Early in his career, Kobe played with Shaquille O'Neal. They won three NBA titles in a row!

After Shaq left the team, Kobe had to score a lot more points. So he did!

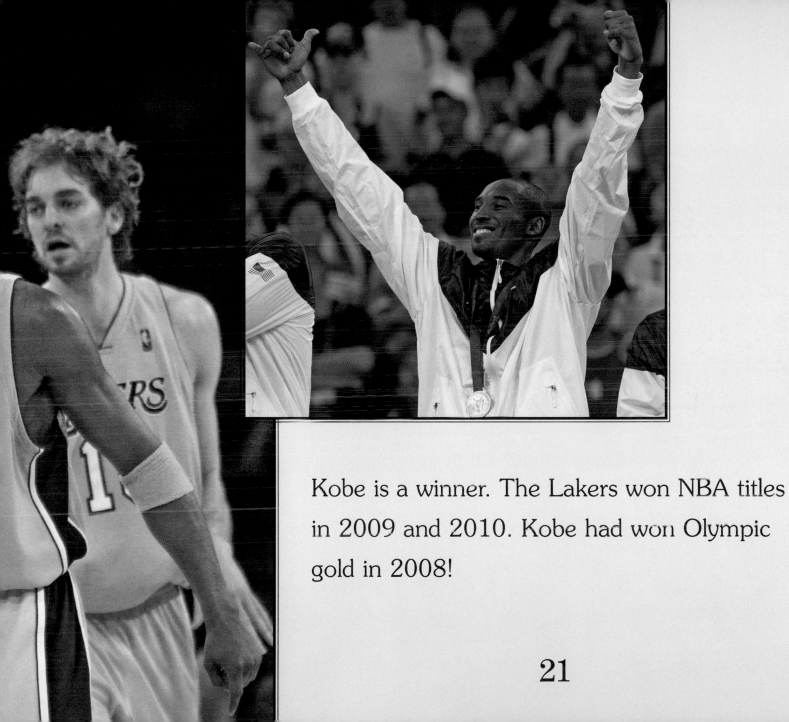

Kobe is a winner. The Lakers won NBA titles in 2009 and 2010. Kobe had won Olympic gold in 2008!

Kobe is looking forward to winning many more trophies!

Further Reading

Bradley, Michael. *Kobe Bryant*. New York.: Benchmark Books, 2003.

Gitlin, Marty. *Kobe Bryant: NBA Champion*. Edina, Minn.: ABDO Publishing Company, 2011

Internet Address

NBA.com—Kobe Bryant

http://www.nba.com/playerfile/kobe_bryant/